GIT

The Ultimate Guide for Beginner
Learn Git Version Control

Jameson Garner

TABLE OF CONTENTS

PART 1: GIT - BASIC CONCEPTS

Version Control System

Version Control System (VCS) is a software that helps software developers to work together and maintain a complete history of their work.

Listed below are the functions of a VCS −

- ❖ Allows developers to work simultaneously.
- ❖ Does not allow overwriting each other's changes.
- ❖ Maintains a history of every version.

Following are the types of VCS –

- ❖ Centralized version control system (CVCS).
- ❖ Distributed/Decentralized version control system (DVCS).

In this chapter, we will concentrate only on distributed version control system and especially on Git. Git falls under distributed version control system.

Distributed Version Control System

Centralized version control system (CVCS) uses a central server to store all files and enables team collaboration. But the major drawback of CVCS is its single point of failure, i.e., failure of the central server. Unfortunately, if the central server goes down for an hour, then during that hour, no one can collaborate at all. And even in a worst case, if the disk of the central server gets corrupted and proper backup has not been taken, then you will lose the entire history of the project. Here, distributed version control system (DVCS) comes into picture.

DVCS clients not only check out the latest snapshot of the directory but they also fully mirror the repository. If the server goes down, then the repository from any client can be copied back to the server to restore it. Every checkout is a full backup of the repository. Git does not rely on the central server and that is why you can perform many operations when you are offline. You can commit changes, create branches, view logs, and perform other operations when you are offline. You require network connection only to publish your changes and take the latest changes.

Advantages of Git

Free and open source

Git is released under GPL's open source license. It is available freely over the internet. You can use Git to manage property projects without paying a single penny. As it is an open source, you can download its source code and also perform changes according to your requirements.

Fast and small

As most of the operations are performed locally, it gives a huge benefit in terms of speed. Git does not rely on the central server; that is why, there is no need to interact with the remote server for every operation. The core part of Git is written in C, which avoids runtime overheads associated with other high-level languages. Though Git mirrors entire repository, the size of the data on the client side is small. This illustrates the efficiency of Git at compressing and storing data on the client side.

Implicit backup

The chances of losing data are very rare when there are multiple copies of it. Data present on any client side mirrors the repository, hence it can be used in the event of a crash or disk corruption.

Security

Git uses a common cryptographic hash function called secure hash function (SHA1), to name and identify objects within its database. Every file and commit is check-summed and retrieved by its checksum at the time of checkout. It implies that, it is impossible to change file, date, and commit message and any other data from the Git database without knowing Git.

No need of powerful hardware

In case of CVCS, the central server needs to be powerful enough to serve requests of the entire team. For smaller teams, it is not an issue, but as the team size grows, the hardware limitations of the server can be a performance bottleneck. In case of DVCS, developers don't interact with the server unless they need to push or pull changes. All the heavy lifting happens on the client side, so the server hardware can be very simple indeed.

Easier branching

CVCS uses cheap copy mechanism, If we create a new branch, it will copy all the codes to the new branch, so it is time-consuming and not efficient. Also, deletion and merging of branches in CVCS is complicated and time-consuming. But branch management with Git is very simple. It takes only a few seconds to create, delete, and merge branches.

DVCS Terminologies

Local Repository

Every VCS tool provides a private workplace as a working copy. Developers make changes in their private workplace and after commit, these changes become a part of the repository. Git takes it one step further by providing them a private copy of the whole repository. Users can perform many operations with this repository such as add file, remove file, rename file, move file, commit changes, and many more.

Working Directory and Staging Area or Index

The working directory is the place where files are checked out. In other CVCS, developers generally make modifications and commit their changes directly to the repository. But Git uses a different strategy. Git doesn't track each and every modified file. Whenever you do commit an operation, Git looks for the files present in the staging area. Only those files present in the staging area are considered for commit and not all the modified files.

Let us see the basic workflow of Git.

Step 1 − You modify a file from the working directory.

Step 2 − You add these files to the staging area.

Step 3 − You perform commit operation that moves the files from the staging area.

After push operation, it stores the changes permanently to the Git repository.

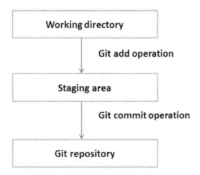

Suppose you modified two files, namely "sort.c" and "search.c" and you want two different commits for each operation. You can add one file in the staging area and do commit. After the first commit, repeat the same procedure for another file.

```
# First commit
[bash]$ git add sort.c
# adds file to the staging area
[bash]$ git commit -m "Added sort operation"
# Second commit
[bash]$ git add search.c
# adds file to the staging area
[bash]$ git commit -m "Added search operation"
```

Blobs

Blob stands for Binary Large Object. Each version of a file is represented by blob. A blob holds the file data but doesn't contain any metadata about the file. It is a binary file, and in Git database, it is named as SHA1 hash of that file. In Git, files are not addressed by names. Everything is content-addressed.

Trees

Tree is an object, which represents a directory. It holds blobs as well as other sub-directories. A tree is a binary file that stores references to blobs and trees which are also named as SHA1 hash of the tree object.

Commits

Commit holds the current state of the repository. A commit is also named by SHA1 hash. You can consider a commit object as a node of the linked list. Every commit object has a pointer to the parent commit object. From a given commit, you can traverse back by looking at the parent pointer to view the history of the commit. If a commit has multiple parent commits, then that particular commit has been created by merging two branches.

Branches

Branches are used to create another line of development. By default, Git has a master branch, which is same as trunk in Subversion. Usually, a branch is created to work on a new feature. Once the feature is completed, it is merged back with the master branch and we delete the branch. Every branch is referenced by HEAD, which points to the latest commit in the branch. Whenever you make a commit, HEAD is updated with the latest commit.

Tags

Tag assigns a meaningful name with a specific version in the repository. Tags are very similar to branches, but the difference is that tags are immutable. It means, tag is a branch, which nobody intends to modify. Once a tag is created for a particular commit, even if you create a new commit, it will not be updated. Usually, developers create tags for product releases.

Clone

Clone operation creates the instance of the repository. Clone operation not only checks out the working copy, but it also mirrors the complete repository. Users can perform many operations with this local repository. The only time networking gets involved is when the repository instances are being synchronized.

Pull

Pull operation copies the changes from a remote repository instance to a local one. The pull operation is used for synchronization between two repository instances. This is same as the update operation in Subversion.

Push

Push operation copies changes from a local repository instance to a remote one. This is used to store the changes permanently into the Git repository. This is same as the commit operation in Subversion.

HEAD

HEAD is a pointer, which always points to the latest commit in the branch. Whenever you make a commit, HEAD is updated with the latest commit. The heads of the branches are stored in .git/refs/heads/ directory.

```
[CentOS]$ ls -1 .git/refs/heads/
master
[CentOS]$ cat .git/refs/heads/master
570837e7d58fa4bccd86cb575d884502188b0c49
```

Revision

Revision represents the version of the source code. Revisions in Git are represented by commits. These commits are identified by SHA1 secure hashes.

URL

URL represents the location of the Git repository. Git URL is stored in config file.

```
[tom@CentOS tom_repo]$ pwd
/home/tom/tom_repo
[tom@CentOS tom_repo]$ cat .git/config
[core]
repositoryformatversion = 0
filemode = true
bare = false
logallrefupdates = true
[remote "origin"]
url = gituser@git.server.com:project.git
fetch = +refs/heads/*:refs/remotes/origin/*
```

PART 2: GIT - ENVIRONMENT SETUP

Before you can use Git, you have to install and do some basic configuration changes. Below are the steps to install Git client on Ubuntu and Centos Linux.

Installation of Git Client

If you are using Debian base GNU/Linux distribution, then apt-get command will do the needful.

```
[ubuntu ~]$ sudo apt-get install git-core
[sudo] password for ubuntu:
[ubuntu ~]$ git --version
git version 1.8.1.2
```

And if you are using RPM based GNU/Linux distribution, then use yum command as given.

```
[CentOS ~]$
su -
Password:
[CentOS ~]# yum -y install git-core
[CentOS ~]# git --version
git version 1.7.1
```

Customize Git Environment

Git provides the git config tool, which allows you to set configuration variables. Git stores all global configurations in .gitconfig file, which is located in your home directory. To set these configuration values as global, add the --global option, and if you omit --global option, then your configurations are specific for the current Git repository.

You can also set up system wide configuration. Git stores these values in the /etc/gitconfig file, which contains the configuration for every user and repository on the system. To set these values, you must have the root rights and use the --system option.

When the above code is compiled and executed, it produces the following result −

Setting username

This information is used by Git for each commit.

```
[jerry@CentOS project]$ git config --global user.name "Jerry Mouse"
```

Setting email id

This information is used by Git for each commit.

```
[jerry@CentOS project]$ git config --global user.email "jerry@tutorialspoint.com"
```

Avoid merge commits for pulling

You pull the latest changes from a remote repository, and if these changes are divergent, then by default Git creates merge commits. We can avoid this via following settings.

```
jerry@CentOS project]$ git config --global branch.autosetuprebase always
```

Color highlighting

The following commands enable color highlighting for Git in the console.

```
[jerry@CentOS project]$ git config --global color.ui true
[jerry@CentOS project]$ git config --global color.status auto
[jerry@CentOS project]$ git config --global color.branch auto
```

Setting default editor

By default, Git uses the system default editor, which is taken from the VISUAL or EDITOR environment variable. We can configure a different one by using git config.

```
[jerry@CentOS project]$ git config --global core.editor vim
```

Setting default merge tool

Git does not provide a default merge tool for integrating conflicting changes into your working tree. We can set default merge tool by enabling following settings.

```
[jerry@CentOS project]$ git config --global merge.tool vimdiff
```

Listing Git settings

To verify your Git settings of the local repository, use git config –list command as given below.

```
[jerry@CentOS ~]$ git config --list
The above command will produce the following result.
user.name=Jerry Mouse
user.email=jerry@tutorialspoint.com
push.default=nothing
branch.autosetuprebase=always
color.ui=true
color.status=auto
color.branch=auto
core.editor=vim
merge.tool=vimdiff
```

PART 3: GIT - LIFE CYCLE

In this chapter, we will discuss the life cycle of Git. In later chapters, we will cover the Git commands for each operation.

GENERAL WORKFLOW IS AS FOLLOWS –

- ❖ You clone the Git repository as a working copy.
- ❖ You modify the working copy by adding/editing files.
- ❖ If necessary, you also update the working copy by taking other developer's changes.
- ❖ You review the changes before commit.
- ❖ You commit changes. If everything is fine, then you push the changes to the repository.
- ❖ After committing, if you realize something is wrong, then you correct the last commit and push the changes to the repository.

Shown below is the pictorial representation of the work-flow.

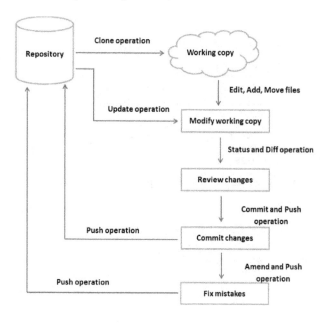

PART 4: GIT - CREATE OPERATION

In this chapter, we will see how to create a remote Git repository; from now on, we will refer to it as Git Server. We need a Git server to allow team collaboration.

Create New User

```
# add new group
[root@CentOS ~]# groupadd dev
# add new user
[root@CentOS ~]# useradd -G devs -d /home/gituser -m -s /bin/bash gituser
# change password
[root@CentOS ~]# passwd gituser
The above command will produce the following result.
Changing password for user gituser.
New password:
Retype new password:
passwd: all authentication token updated successfully.
```

Create a Bare Repository

Let us initialize a new repository by using init command followed by --bare option. It initializes the repository without a working directory. By convention, the bare repository must be named as .git.

```
[gituser@CentOS ~]$ pwd
/home/gituser
[gituser@CentOS ~]$ mkdir project.git
[gituser@CentOS ~]$ cd project.git/
[gituser@CentOS project.git]$ ls
[gituser@CentOS project.git]$ git --bare init
Initialized empty Git repository in /home/gituser-m/project.git/
[gituser@CentOS project.git]$ ls
branches config description HEAD hooks info objects refs
```

Generate Public/Private RSA Key Pair

Let us walk through the process of configuring a Git server, ssh-keygen utility generates public/private RSA key pair, that we will use for user authentication.

Open a terminal and enter the following command and just press enter for each input. After successful completion, it will create a .ssh directory inside the home directory.

```
tom@CentOS ~]$ pwd
/home/tom
[tom@CentOS ~]$ ssh-keygen
The above command will produce the following result.
Generating public/private rsa key pair.
Enter file in which to save the key (/home/tom/.ssh/id_rsa): Press Enter Only
Created directory '/home/tom/.ssh'.
Enter passphrase (empty for no passphrase): --------------> Press Enter Only
Enter same passphrase again: ---------------------------> Press Enter Only
Your identification has been saved in /home/tom/.ssh/id_rsa.
Your public key has been saved in /home/tom/.ssh/id_rsa.pub.
The key fingerprint is:
df:93:8c:a1:b8:b7:67:69:3a:1f:65:e8:0e:e9:25:a1 tom@CentOS
The key's randomart image is:
+--[ RSA 2048]----+
|                 |
|                 |
|                 |
|                 |
|  Soo |          |
|  o*B. |         |
|  E = *.= |      |
|  oo==. . |      |
|  ..+Oo          |
|                 |
+-----------------+
```

ssh-keygen has generated two keys, first one is private (i.e., id_rsa) and the second one is public (i.e., id_rsa.pub).

Note: Never share your PRIVATE KEY with others.

Adding Keys to authorized_keys

Suppose there are two developers working on a project, namely Tom and Jerry. Both users have generated public keys. Let us see how to use these keys for authentication.

Tom added his public key to the server by using ssh-copy-id command as given below –

```
[tom@CentOS ~]$ pwd
/home/tom
[tom@CentOS ~]$ ssh-copy-id -i ~/.ssh/id_rsa.pub gituser@git.server.com
The above command will produce the following result.
gituser@git.server.com's password:
Now try logging into the machine, with "ssh 'gituser@git.server.com'", and check in:
.ssh/authorized_keys
to make sure we haven't added extra keys that you weren't expecting.
Similarly, Jerry added his public key to the server by using ssh-copy-id command.
[jerry@CentOS ~]$ pwd
/home/jerry
[jerry@CentOS ~]$ ssh-copy-id -i ~/.ssh/id_rsa gituser@git.server.com
```

The above command will produce the following result.

```
gituser@git.server.com's password:
Now try logging into the machine, with "ssh 'gituser@git.server.com'", and check in:
.ssh/authorized_keys
to make sure we haven't added extra keys that you weren't expecting.
```

Push Changes to the Repository

We have created a bare repository on the server and allowed access for two users. From now on, Tom and Jerry can push their changes to the repository by adding it as a remote.

Git init command creates .git directory to store metadata about the repository every time it reads the configuration from the .git/config file.

Tom creates a new directory, adds README file, and commits his change as initial commit. After commit, he verifies the commit message by running the git log command.

```
[tom@CentOS ~]$ pwd
/home/tom
[tom@CentOS ~]$ mkdir tom_repo
[tom@CentOS ~]$ cd tom_repo/
[tom@CentOS tom_repo]$ git init
Initialized empty Git repository in /home/tom/tom_repo/.git/
[tom@CentOS tom_repo]$ echo 'TODO: Add contents for README' > README
[tom@CentOS tom_repo]$ git status -s
?? README
[tom@CentOS tom_repo]$ git add .
[tom@CentOS tom_repo]$ git status -s
A README
[tom@CentOS tom_repo]$ git commit -m 'Initial commit'
```

The above command will produce the following result.

```
[master (root-commit) 19ae206] Initial commit
1 files changed, 1 insertions(+), 0 deletions(-)
create mode 100644 README
```

Tom checks the log message by executing the git log command.

```
[tom@CentOS tom_repo]$ git log
```

The above command will produce the following result.

```
commit 19ae20683fc460db7d127cf201a1429523b0e319
Author: Tom Cat <tom@tutorialspoint.com>
Date: Wed Sep 11 07:32:56 2013 +0530
Initial commit
```

Tom committed his changes to the local repository. Now, it's time to push the changes to the remote repository. But before that, we have to add the repository as a remote, this is a one-time operation. After this, he can safely push the changes to the remote repository.

Note − By default, Git pushes only to matching branches: For every branch that exists on the local side, the remote side is updated if a branch with the same name already exists there. In our tutorials, every time we push changes to the origin master branch, use appropriate branch name according to your requirement.

```
[tom@CentOS tom_repo]$ git remote add origin gituser@git.server.com:project.git
[tom@CentOS tom_repo]$ git push origin master
```

The above command will produce the following result.

```
Counting objects: 3, done.
Writing objects: 100% (3/3), 242 bytes, done.
Total 3 (delta 0), reused 0 (delta 0)
To gituser@git.server.com:project.git
* [new branch]
master -> master
```

Now, the changes are successfully committed to the remote repository.

PART 5: GIT - CLONE OPERATION

We have a bare repository on the Git server and Tom also pushed his first version. Now, Jerry can view his changes. The Clone operation creates an instance of the remote repository.

Jerry creates a new directory in his home directory and performs the clone operation.

```
[jerry@CentOS ~]$ mkdir jerry_repo
[jerry@CentOS ~]$ cd jerry_repo/
[jerry@CentOS jerry_repo]$ git clone gituser@git.server.com:project.git
```

The above command will produce the following result.

```
Initialized empty Git repository in /home/jerry/jerry_repo/project/.git/
remote: Counting objects: 3, done.
Receiving objects: 100% (3/3), 241 bytes, done.
remote: Total 3 (delta 0), reused 0 (delta 0)
```

Jerry changes the directory to new local repository and lists its directory contents.

```
[jerry@CentOS jerry_repo]$ cd project/
[jerry@CentOS jerry_repo]$ ls
README
```

PART 6: GIT - PERFORM CHANGES

Jerry clones the repository and decides to implement basic string operations. So he creates string.c file. After adding the contents, string.c will look like as follows —

```c
#include <stdio.h>

int my_strlen(char*s)
{
char*p = s;
while(*p)
++p;
return(p - s);
}
int main(void)
{
int i;
char*s[]=
{
"Git tutorials",
"Tutorials Point"
};

for(i =0; i <2;++i)

 printf("string lenght of %s = %d\n", s[i], my_strlen(s[i]));
return 0;
}
```

He compiled and tested his code and everything is working fine. Now, he can safely add these changes to the repository.

Git add operation adds file to the staging area.

```
[jerry@CentOS project]$ git status -s
?? string
?? string.c
[jerry@CentOS project]$ git add string.c
```

Git is showing a question mark before file names. Obviously, these files are not a part of Git, and that is why Git does not know what to do with these files. That is why, Git is showing a question mark before file names.

Jerry has added the file to the stash area, git status command will show files present in the staging area.

```
[jerry@CentOS project]$ git status -s
A string.c
?? string
```

To commit the changes, he used the git commit command followed by —m option. If we omit —m option. Git will open a text editor where we can write multiline commit message.

```
[jerry@CentOS project]$ git commit -m 'Implemented my_strlen function'
```

The above command will produce the following result —

```
[master cbe1249] Implemented my_strlen function
1 files changed, 24 insertions(+), 0 deletions(-)
create mode 100644 string.c
```

After commit to view log details, he runs the git log command. It will display the information of all the commits with their commit ID, commit author, commit date and SHA-1 hash of commit.

```
[jerry@CentOS project]$ git log
The above command will produce the following result -
commit cbe1249b140dad24b2c35b15cc7e26a6f02d2277
Author: Jerry Mouse <jerry@tutorialspoint.com>
Date: Wed Sep 11 08:05:26 2013 +0530
Implemented my_strlen function
commit 19ae20683fc460db7d127cf201a1429523b0e319
Author: Tom Cat <tom@tutorialspoint.com>
Date: Wed Sep 11 07:32:56 2013 +0530
Initial commit
```

PART 7: GIT - REVIEW CHANGES

After viewing the commit details, Jerry realizes that the string length cannot be negative, that's why he decides to change the return type of my_strlen function.

Jerry uses the git log command to view log details.

```
[jerry@CentOS project]$ git log
```

The above command will produce the following result.

```
commit cbe1249b140dad24b2c35b15cc7e26a6f02d2277
Author: Jerry Mouse <jerry@tutorialspoint.com>
Date: Wed Sep 11 08:05:26 2013 +0530
Implemented my_strlen functio
```

Jerry uses the git show command to view the commit details. The git show command takes SHA-1 commit ID as a parameter.

```
[jerry@CentOS project]$ git show cbe1249b140dad24b2c35b15cc7e26a6f02d2277
```

The above command will produce the following result −

```
commit cbe1249b140dad24b2c35b15cc7e26a6f02d2277
Author: Jerry Mouse <jerry@tutorialspoint.com>
Date: Wed Sep 11 08:05:26 2013 +0530
Implemented my_strlen function
diff --git a/string.c b/string.c
new file mode 100644
index 0000000..187afb9
--- /dev/null
+++ b/string.c
@@ -0,0 +1,24 @@
+#include <stdio.h>
+
+int my_strlen(char *s)
+{
+
+ char *p = s;
+
+
+ while (*p)
+ ++p;
+ return (p -s );
+
+}
+
```

He changes the return type of the function from int to size_t. After testing the code, he reviews his changes by running the git diff command.

```
[jerry@CentOS project]$ git diff
```

The above command will produce the following result −

16

```
diff --git a/string.c b/string.c
index 187afb9..7da2992 100644
--- a/string.c
+++ b/string.c
@@ -1,6 +1,6 @@
#include <stdio.h>
-int my_strlen(char *s)
+size_t my_strlen(char *s)
{
 char *p = s;
@@ -18,7 +18,7 @@ int main(void)
};
for (i = 0; i < 2; ++i)
{
- printf("string lenght of %s = %d\n", s[i], my_strlen(s[i]));
+ printf("string lenght of %s = %lu\n", s[i], my_strlen(s[i]));
 return 0;
}
```

Git diff shows '+' sign before lines, which are newly added and '−' for deleted lines.

PART 8: GIT - COMMIT CHANGES

Jerry has already committed the changes and he wants to correct his last commit. In this case, git amend operation will help. The amend operation changes the last commit including your commit message; it creates a new commit ID.

Before amend operation, he checks the commit log.

```
[jerry@CentOS project]$ git log
```

The above command will produce the following result.

```
commit cbe1249b140dad24b2c35b15cc7e26a6f02d2277
Author: Jerry Mouse <jerry@tutorialspoint.com>
Date: Wed Sep 11 08:05:26 2013 +0530
Implemented my_strlen function
commit 19ae20683fc460db7d127cf201a1429523b0e319
Author: Tom Cat <tom@tutorialspoint.com>
Date: Wed Sep 11 07:32:56 2013 +0530
Initial commit
```

Jerry commits the new changes with -- amend operation and views the commit log.

```
[jerry@CentOS project]$ git status -s
M string.c
?? string
[jerry@CentOS project]$ git add string.c
[jerry@CentOS project]$ git status -s
M string.c
?? string
[jerry@CentOS project]$ git commit --amend -m 'Changed return type of my_strlen to size_t
[master d1e19d3] Changed return type of my_strlen to size_t
1 files changed, 24 insertions(+), 0 deletions(-)
create mode 100644 string.c
```

Now, git log will show new commit message with new commit ID −

```
[jerry@CentOS project]$ git log
```

The above command will produce the following result.

```
commit d1e19d316224cddc437e3ed34ec3c931ad803958
Author: Jerry Mouse <jerry@tutorialspoint.com>
Date: Wed Sep 11 08:05:26 2013 +0530
Changed return type of my_strlen to size_t
commit 19ae20683fc460db7d127cf201a1429523b0e319
Author: Tom Cat <tom@tutorialspoint.com>
Date: Wed Sep 11 07:32:56 2013 +0530
Initial commit
```

PART 9: GIT - PUSH OPERATION

Jerry modified his last commit by using the amend operation and he is ready to push the changes. The Push operation stores data permanently to the Git repository. After a successful push operation, other developers can see Jerry's changes.

He executes the git log command to view the commit details.

```
[jerry@CentOS project]$ git log
```

The above command will produce the following result:

```
commit d1e19d316224cddc437e3ed34ec3c931ad803958
Author: Jerry Mouse <jerry@tutorialspoint.com>
Date: Wed Sep 11 08:05:26 2013 +0530
Changed return type of my_strlen to size_t
```

Before push operation, he wants to review his changes, so he uses the git show command to review his changes.

```
[jerry@CentOS project]$ git show d1e19d316224cddc437e3ed34ec3c931ad803958
```

The above command will produce the following result:

```
commit d1e19d316224cddc437e3ed34ec3c931ad803958
Author: Jerry Mouse <jerry@tutorialspoint.com>
Date: Wed Sep 11 08:05:26 2013 +0530
Changed return type of my_strlen to size_t
diff --git a/string.c b/string.c
new file mode 100644
index 0000000..7da2992
--- /dev/null
+++ b/string.c
@@ -0,0 +1,24 @@
+#include <stdio.h>
+
+size_t my_strlen(char *s)
+
{
 +
 char *p = s;
 +
 +
 while (*p)
 + ++p;
 + return (p -s );
 +
}
+
+int main(void)
+
{
 + int i;
 + char *s[] =
 {
 + "Git tutorials",
 + "Tutorials Point"
 +
 };
 +
 +
 +
 for (i = 0; i < 2; ++i)
 printf("string lenght of %s = %lu\n", s[i], my_strlen(s[i]));
 +
 +
 return 0;
 +
}
```

Jerry is happy with his changes and he is ready to push his changes.

```
[jerry@CentOS project]$ git push origin master
```

The above command will produce the following result:

```
Counting objects: 4, done.
Compressing objects: 100% (3/3), done.
Writing objects: 100% (3/3), 517 bytes, done.
Total 3 (delta 0), reused 0 (delta 0)
To gituser@git.server.com:project.git
19ae206..d1e19d3 master -> master
```

Jerry's changes have been successfully pushed to the repository; now other developers can view his changes by performing clone or update operation.

PART 10: GIT - UPDATE OPERATION

Modify Existing Function

Tom performs the clone operation and finds a new file string.c. He wants to know who added this file to the repository and for what purpose, so, he executes the git log command.

```
[tom@CentOS ~]$ git clone gituser@git.server.com:project.git
```

The above command will produce the following result −

```
Initialized empty Git repository in /home/tom/project/.git/
remote: Counting objects: 6, done.
remote: Compressing objects: 100% (4/4), done.
Receiving objects: 100% (6/6), 726 bytes, done.
remote: Total 6 (delta 0), reused 0 (delta 0)
```

The Clone operation will create a new directory inside the current working directory. He changes the directory to newly created directory and executes the git log command.

```
[tom@CentOS ~]$ cd project/
[tom@CentOS project]$ git log
```

The above command will produce the following result −

```
commit d1e19d316224cddc437e3ed34ec3c931ad803958
Author: Jerry Mouse <jerry@tutorialspoint.com>
Date: Wed Sep 11 08:05:26 2013 +0530
Changed return type of my_strlen to size_t
commit 19ae20683fc460db7d127cf201a1429523b0e319
Author: Tom Cat <tom@tutorialspoint.com>
Date: Wed Sep 11 07:32:56 2013 +0530
Initial commit
```

After observing the log, he realizes that the file string.c was added by Jerry to implement basic string operations. He is curious about Jerry's code. So he opens string.c in text editor and immediately finds a bug. In my_strlen function, Jerry is not using a constant pointer. So, he decides to modify Jerry's code. After modification, the code looks as follows −

```
[tom@CentOS project]$ git diff
```

The above command will produce the following result −

```
diff --git a/string.c b/string.c
index 7da2992..32489eb 100644
--- a/string.c
+++ b/string.c
@@ -1,8 +1,8 @@
#include <stdio.h>
-size_t my_strlen(char *s)
+size_t my_strlen(const char *s)
{
- char *p = s;
+ const char *p = s;
while (*p)
++p;
}
```

After testing, he commits his change.

```
[tom@CentOS project]$ git status -s
M string.c
?? string
[tom@CentOS project]$ git add string.c
[tom@CentOS project]$ git commit -m 'Changed char pointer to const char pointer'
[master cea2c00] Changed char pointer to const char pointer
1 files changed, 2 insertions(+), 2 deletions(-)
[tom@CentOS project]$ git log
```

The above command will produce the following result −

```
commit cea2c000f53ba99508c5959e3e12fff493b
Author: Tom Cat <tom@tutorialspoint.com>
Date: Wed Sep 11 08:32:07 2013 +0530
Changed char pointer to const char pointer
commit d1e19d316224cddc437e3ed34ec3c931ad803958
Author: Jerry Mouse <jerry@tutorialspoint.com>
Date: Wed Sep 11 08:05:26 2013 +0530
Changed return type of my_strlen to size_t
commit 19ae20683fc460db7d127cf201a1429523b0e319
Author: Tom Cat <tom@tutorialspoint.com>
Date: Wed Sep 11 07:32:56 2013 +0530
Initial commit
```

Tom uses git push command to push his changes.

```
[tom@CentOS project]$ git push origin master
```

The above command will produce the following result −

```
Counting objects: 5, done.
Compressing objects: 100% (3/3), done.
Writing objects: 100% (3/3), 336 bytes, done.
Total 3 (delta 1), reused 0 (delta 0)
To gituser@git.server.com:project.git
d1e19d3..cea2c00 master -> master
```

Add New Function

Meanwhile, Jerry decides to implement string compare functionality. So he modifies string.c. After modification, the file looks as follows −

```
[jerry@CentOS project]$ git diff
```

The above command will produce the following result −

```
index 7da2992..bc864ed 100644
--- a/string.c
+++ b/string.c
30Git Tutorials
@@ -9,9 +9,20 @@ size_t my_strlen(char *s)
return (p -s );
}
+char *my_strcpy(char *t, char *s)
+
{
+
 char *p = t;
+
+ while (*t++ = *s++)
+ ;
+
+
 return p;
+
}
+
int main(void)
{
 int i;
+
 char p1[32];
 char *s[] =
{
"Git tutorials",
"Tutorials Point"
@@ -20,5 +31,7 @@ int main(void)
for (i = 0; i < 2; ++i)
printf("string lenght of %s = %lu\n", s[i], my_strlen(s[i]));
+
printf("%s\n", my_strcpy(p1, "Hello, World !!!"));
+
 return 0;
 }
}
```

After testing, he is ready to push his change.

```
[jerry@CentOS project]$ git status -s
M string.c
?? string
[jerry@CentOS project]$ git add string.c
[jerry@CentOS project]$ git commit -m "Added my_strcpy function"
[master e944e5a] Added my_strcpy function
1 files changed, 13 insertions(+), 0 deletions(-)
```

Before push operation, he verifies commit by viewing log messages.

```
[jerry@CentOS project]$ git log
```
The
above command will produce the following result −

```
commit e944e5aab74b26e7447d3281b225309e4e59efcd
Author: Jerry Mouse <jerry@tutorialspoint.com>
Date: Wed Sep 11 08:41:42 2013 +0530
Added my_strcpy function
commit d1e19d316224cddc437e3ed34ec3c931ad803958
Author: Jerry Mouse <jerry@tutorialspoint.com>
Date: Wed Sep 11 08:05:26 2013 +0530
Changed return type of my_strlen to size_t
commit 19ae20683fc460db7d127cf201a1429523b0e319
Author: Tom Cat <tom@tutorialspoint.com>
Date: Wed Sep 11 07:32:56 2013 +0530
Initial commit
```

Jerry is happy with the changes and he wants to push his changes.

```
[jerry@CentOS project]$ git push origin master
```

The above command will produce the following result —

```
To gituser@git.server.com:project.git
! [rejected]
master -> master (non-fast-forward)
error: failed to push some refs to 'gituser@git.server.com:project.git'
To prevent you from losing history, non-fast-forward updates were rejected
Merge the remote changes before pushing again. See the 'Note about
fast-forwards' section of 'git push --help' for details.
```

But Git is not allowing Jerry to push his changes. Because Git identified that remote repository and Jerry's local repository are not in sync. Because of this, he can lose the history of the project. To avoid this mess, Git failed this operation. Now, Jerry has to first update the local repository and only thereafter, he can push his own changes.

Fetch Latest Changes

Jerry executes the git pull command to synchronize his local repository with the remote one.

```
[jerry@CentOS project]$ git pull
```

The above command will produce the following result —

```
remote: Counting objects: 5, done.
remote: Compressing objects: 100% (3/3), done.
remote: Total 3 (delta 1), reused 0 (delta 0)
Unpacking objects: 100% (3/3), done.
From git.server.com:project
d1e19d3..cea2c00 master -> origin/master
First, rewinding head to replay your work on top of it...
Applying: Added my_strcpy function
```

After pull operation, Jerry checks the log messages and finds the details of Tom's commit with commit ID cea2c000f53ba99508c5959e3e12fff493ba6f69

```
[jerry@CentOS project]$ git log
```

The above command will produce the following result —

```
commit e86f0621c2a3f68190bba633a9fe6c57c94f8e4f
Author: Jerry Mouse <jerry@tutorialspoint.com>
Date: Wed Sep 11 08:41:42 2013 +0530
Added my_strcpy function
commit cea2c000f53ba99508c5959e3e12fff493ba6f69
Author: Tom Cat <tom@tutorialspoint.com>
Date: Wed Sep 11 08:32:07 2013 +0530
Changed char pointer to const char pointer
commit d1e19d316224cddc437e3ed34ec3c931ad803958
Author: Jerry Mouse <jerry@tutorialspoint.com>
Date: Wed Sep 11 08:05:26 2013 +0530
Changed return type of my_strlen to size_t
commit 19ae20683fc460db7d127cf201a1429523b0e319
Author: Tom Cat <tom@tutorialspoint.com>
Date: Wed Sep 11 07:32:56 2013 +0530
Initial commit
```

Now, Jerry's local repository is fully synchronized with the remote repository. So he can safely push his changes.

```
[jerry@CentOS project]$ git push origin master
```

The above command will produce the following result −

```
Counting objects: 5, done.
Compressing objects: 100% (3/3), done.
Writing objects: 100% (3/3), 455 bytes, done.
Total 3 (delta 1), reused 0 (delta 0)
To gituser@git.server.com:project.git
cea2c00..e86f062 master -> master
```

PART 11: GIT - STASH OPERATION

Suppose you are implementing a new feature for your product. Your code is in progress and suddenly a customer escalation comes. Because of this, you have to keep aside your new feature work for a few hours. You cannot commit your partial code and also cannot throw away your changes. So you need some temporary space, where you can store your partial changes and later on commit it.

In Git, the stash operation takes your modified tracked files, stages changes, and saves them on a stack of unfinished changes that you can reapply at any time.

```
[jerry@CentOS project]$ git status -s
M string.c
?? string
```

Now, you want to switch branches for customer escalation, but you don't want to commit what you've been working on yet; so you'll stash the changes. To push a new stash onto your stack, run the git stash command.

```
[jerry@CentOS project]$ git stash
Saved working directory and index state WIP on master: e86f062 Added my_strcpy function
HEAD is now at e86f062 Added my_strcpy function
```

Now, your working directory is clean and all the changes are saved on a stack. Let us verify it with the git status command.

```
[jerry@CentOS project]$ git status -s
?? string
```

Now you can safely switch the branch and work elsewhere. We can view a list of stashed changes by using the git stash list command.

```
[jerry@CentOS project]$ git stash list
stash@{0}: WIP on master: e86f062 Added my_strcpy function
```

Suppose you have resolved the customer escalation and you are back on your new feature looking for your half-done code, just execute the git stash pop command, to remove the changes from the stack and place them in the current working directory.

```
[jerry@CentOS project]$ git status -s
?? string
[jerry@CentOS project]$ git stash pop
```

The above command will produce the following result:

```
# On branch master
# Changed but not updated:
# (use "git add ..." to update what will be committed)
# (use "git checkout -- ..." to discard changes in working directory)
#
#
modified: string.c
#
# Untracked files:
# (use "git add ..." to include in what will be committed)
#
#
string
no changes added to commit (use "git add" and/or "git commit -a")
Dropped refs/stash@{0} (36f79dfedae4ac20e2e8558830154bd6315e72d4)
[jerry@CentOS project]$ git status -s
M string.c
?? string
```

PART 12: GIT - MOVE OPERATION

As the name suggests, the move operation moves a directory or a file from one location to another. Tom decides to move the source code into src directory. The modified directory structure will appear as follows —

```
[tom@CentOS project]$ pwd
/home/tom/project
[tom@CentOS project]$ ls
README string string.c
[tom@CentOS project]$ mkdir src
[tom@CentOS project]$ git mv string.c src/
[tom@CentOS project]$ git status -s
R string.c -> src/string.c
?? string
```

To make these changes permanent, we have to push the modified directory structure to the remote repository so that other developers can see this.

```
[tom@CentOS project]$ git commit -m "Modified directory structure"
[master 7d9ea97] Modified directory structure
1 files changed, 0 insertions(+), 0 deletions(-)
rename string.c => src/string.c (100%)
[tom@CentOS project]$ git push origin master
Counting objects: 4, done.
Compressing objects: 100% (2/2), done.
Writing objects: 100% (3/3), 320 bytes, done.
Total 3 (delta 0), reused 0 (delta 0)
To gituser@git.server.com:project.git
e86f062..7d9ea97 master -> master
```

In Jerry's local repository, before the pull operation, it will show the old directory structure.

```
[jerry@CentOS project]$ pwd
/home/jerry/jerry_repo/project
[jerry@CentOS project]$ ls
README string string.c
e86f062..7d9ea97 master -> master
```

But after the pull operation, the directory structure will get updated. Now, Jerry can see the src directory and the file present inside that directory.

```
[jerry@CentOS project]$ git pull
remote: Counting objects: 4, done.
remote: Compressing objects: 100% (2/2), done.
remote: Total 3 (delta 0), reused 0 (delta 0)
Unpacking objects: 100% (3/3), done.
From git.server.com:project
e86f062..7d9ea97 master -> origin/master
First, rewinding head to replay your work on top of it...
Fast-forwarded master to 7d9ea97683da90bcdb87c28ec9b4f64160673c8a.
[jerry@CentOS project]$ ls
README src string
[jerry@CentOS project]$ ls src/
string.c
```

PART 13: GIT - RENAME OPERATION

Till now, both Tom and Jerry were using manual commands to compile their project. Now, Jerry decides to create Makefile for their project and also give a proper name to the file "string.c".

```
[jerry@CentOS project]$ pwd
/home/jerry/jerry_repo/project
[jerry@CentOS project]$ ls
README src
[jerry@CentOS project]$ cd src/
[jerry@CentOS src]$ git add Makefile
[jerry@CentOS src]$ git mv string.c string_operations.c
[jerry@CentOS src]$ git status -s
A Makefile
R string.c -> string_operations.c
```

Git is showing R before file name to indicate that the file has been renamed. For commit operation, Jerry used -a flag, that makes git commit automatically detect the modified files.

```
[jerry@CentOS src]$ git commit -a -m 'Added Makefile and renamed strings.c to
string_operations.c
[master 94f7b26] Added Makefile and renamed strings.c to string_operations.c
1 files changed, 0 insertions(+), 0 deletions(-)
create mode 100644 src/Makefile
rename src/{string.c => string_operations.c} (100%)
```

After commit, he pushes his changes to the repository.

```
[jerry@CentOS src]$ git push origin master
```

The above command will produce the following result —

```
Counting objects: 6, done.
Compressing objects: 100% (3/3), done.
Writing objects: 100% (4/4), 396 bytes, done.
Total 4 (delta 0), reused 0 (delta 0)
To gituser@git.server.com:project.git
7d9ea97..94f7b26 master -> master
```

Now, other developers can view these modifications by updating their local repository.

PART 14: GIT - DELETE OPERATION

Tom updates his local repository and finds the compiled binary in the src directory. After viewing the commit message, he realizes that the compiled binary was added by Jerry.

```
[tom@CentOS src]$ pwd
/home/tom/project/src
[tom@CentOS src]$ ls
Makefile string_operations string_operations.c
[tom@CentOS src]$ file string_operations
string_operations: ELF 64-bit LSB executable, x86-64, version 1 (SYSV), dynamically linked (uses
shared libs), for GNU/Linux 2.6.18, not stripped
[tom@CentOS src]$ git log
commit 29af9d45947dc044e33d69b9141d8d2dad37cc62
Author: Jerry Mouse <jerry@tutorialspoint.com>
Date: Wed Sep 11 10:16:25 2013 +0530
Added compiled binary
```

VCS is used to store the source code only and not executable binaries. So, Tom decides to remove this file from the repository. For further operation, he uses the git rm command.

```
[tom@CentOS src]$ ls
Makefile string_operations string_operations.c
[tom@CentOS src]$ git rm string_operations
rm 'src/string_operations'
[tom@CentOS src]$ git commit -a -m "Removed executable binary"
[master 5776472] Removed executable binary
1 files changed, 0 insertions(+), 0 deletions(-)
delete mode 100755 src/string_operations
```

After commit, he pushes his changes to the repository.

```
[tom@CentOS src]$ git push origin master
delete mode 100755 src/string_operations
```

The above command will produce the following result.

```
Counting objects: 5, done.
Compressing objects: 100% (3/3), done.
Writing objects: 100% (3/3), 310 bytes, done.
Total 3 (delta 1), reused 0 (delta 0)
To gituser@git.server.com:project.git
29af9d4..5776472 master -> master
```

PART 15: GIT - FIX MISTAKES

To err is human. So every VCS provides a feature to fix mistakes until a certain point. Git provides a feature that we can use to undo the modifications that have been made to the local repository.

Suppose the user accidentally does some changes to his local repository and then wants to undo these changes. In such cases, the revert operation plays an important role.

Revert Uncommitted Changes

Let us suppose Jerry accidentally modifies a file from his local repository. But he wants to undo his modification. To handle this situation, we can use the git checkout command. We can use this command to revert the contents of a file.

```
[jerry@CentOS src]$ pwd
/home/jerry/jerry_repo/project/src
[jerry@CentOS src]$ git status -s
M string_operations.c
[jerry@CentOS src]$ git checkout string_operations.c
[jerry@CentOS src]$ git status -s
```

Further, we can use the git checkout command to obtain a deleted file from the local repository. Let us suppose Tom deletes a file from the local repository and we want this file back. We can achieve this by using the same command.

```
[tom@CentOS src]$ pwd
/home/tom/top_repo/project/src
[tom@CentOS src]$ ls -l
Makefile
string_operations.c
[tom@CentOS src]$ rm string_operations.c
[tom@CentOS src]$ ls -l
Makefile
[tom@CentOS src]$ git status -s
D string_operations.c
```

Git is showing the letter D before the filename. This indicates that the file has been deleted from the local repository.

```
[tom@CentOS src]$ git checkout string_operations.c
[tom@CentOS src]$ ls -l
Makefile
string_operations.c
[tom@CentOS src]$ git status -s
```

Note − We can perform all these operations before commit.

Remove Changes from Staging Area

We have seen that when we perform an add operation, the files move from the local repository to the stating area. If a user accidently modifies a file and adds it into the staging area, he can revert his changes, by using the git checkout command.

In Git, there is one HEAD pointer that always points to the latest commit. If you want to undo a change from the staged area, then you can use the git checkout command, but with the checkout command, you have to provide an additional parameter, i.e., the HEAD pointer. The additional commit pointer parameter instructs the git checkout command to reset the working tree and also to remove the staged changes.

Let us suppose Tom modifies a file from his local repository. If we view the status of this file, it will show that the file was modified but not added into the staging area.

```
tom@CentOS src]$ pwd
/home/tom/top_repo/project/src
# Unmodified file
[tom@CentOS src]$ git status -s
# Modify file and view it's status.
[tom@CentOS src]$ git status -s
M string_operations.c
[tom@CentOS src]$ git add string_operations.c
```

Git status shows that the file is present in the staging area, now revert it by using the git checkout command and view the status of the reverted file.

```
[tom@CentOS src]$ git checkout HEAD -- string_operations.c
[tom@CentOS src]$ git status -s
```

Move HEAD Pointer with Git Reset

After doing few changes, you may decide to remove these changes. The Git reset command is used to reset or revert changes. We can perform three different types of reset operations.

Below diagram shows the pictorial representation of Git reset command.

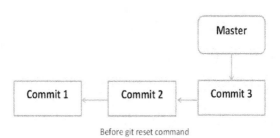

Before git reset command

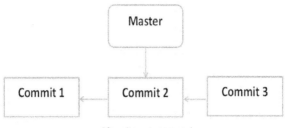

After git reset command

Soft

Each branch has a HEAD pointer, which points to the latest commit. If we use Git reset command with --soft option followed by commit ID, then it will reset the HEAD pointer only without destroying anything.

.git/refs/heads/master file stores the commit ID of the HEAD pointer. We can verify it by using the git log -1 command.

```
[jerry@CentOS project]$ cat .git/refs/heads/master
577647211ed44fe2ae479427a0668a4f12ed71a1
```

Now, view the latest commit ID, which will match with the above commit ID.

```
[jerry@CentOS project]$ git log -2
```

The above command will produce the following result.

```
commit 577647211ed44fe2ae479427a0668a4f12ed71a1
Author: Tom Cat <tom@tutorialspoint.com>
Date: Wed Sep 11 10:21:20 2013 +0530
Removed executable binary
commit 29af9d45947dc044e33d69b9141d8d2dad37cc62
Author: Jerry Mouse <jerry@tutorialspoint.com>
Date: Wed Sep 11 10:16:25 2013 +0530
Added compiled binary
```

Let us reset the HEAD pointer.

```
[jerry@CentOS project]$ git reset --soft HEAD~
```

Now, we just reset the HEAD pointer back by one position. Let us check the contents of .git/refs/heads/master file.

```
[jerry@CentOS project]$ cat .git/refs/heads/master
29af9d45947dc044e33d69b9141d8d2dad37cc62
```

Commit ID from file is changed, now verify it by viewing commit messages.

```
                    jerry@CentOS project]$ git log -2
```

The above command will produce the following result.

```
            commit 29af9d45947dc044e33d69b9141d8d2dad37cc62
            Author: Jerry Mouse <jerry@tutorialspoint.com>
            Date: Wed Sep 11 10:16:25 2013 +0530
            Added compiled binary
            commit 94f7b26005f856f1a1b733ad438e97a0cd509c1a
            Author: Jerry Mouse <jerry@tutorialspoint.com>
            Date: Wed Sep 11 10:08:01 2013 +0530
            Added Makefile and renamed strings.c to string_operations.c
```

mixed

Git reset with --mixed option reverts those changes from the staging area that have not been committed yet. It reverts the changes from the staging area only. The actual changes made to the working copy of the file are unaffected. The default Git reset is equivalent to the git reset -- mixed.

hard

If you use --hard option with the Git reset command, it will clear the staging area; it will reset the HEAD pointer to the latest commit of the specific commit ID and delete the local file changes too.

Let us check the commit ID.

```
                [jerry@CentOS src]$ pwd
                /home/jerry/jerry_repo/project/src
                [jerry@CentOS src]$ git log -1
```

The above command will produce the following result.

```
            commit 577647211ed44fe2ae479427a0668a4f12ed71a1
            Author: Tom Cat <tom@tutorialspoint.com>
            Date: Wed Sep 11 10:21:20 2013 +0530
            Removed executable binary
```

Jerry modified a file by adding single-line comment at the start of file.

```
            [jerry@CentOS src]$ head -2 string_operations.c
            /* This line be removed by git reset operation */
            #include <stdio.h>
```

He verified it by using the git status command.

```
                [jerry@CentOS src]$ git status -s
                M string_operations.c
```

Jerry adds the modified file to the staging area and verifies it with the git status command.

```
[jerry@CentOS src]$ git add string_operations.c
[jerry@CentOS src]$ git status
```

The above command will produce the following result.

```
# On branch master
# Changes to be committed:
# (use "git reset HEAD <file>..." to unstage)
#
#
modified: string_operations.c
#
```

Git status is showing that the file is present in the staging area. Now, reset HEAD with -- hard option.

```
[jerry@CentOS src]$ git reset --hard 577647211ed44fe2ae479427a0668a4f12ed71a1
HEAD is now at 5776472 Removed executable binary
```

Git reset command succeeded, which will revert the file from the staging area as well as remove any local changes made to the file.

```
[jerry@CentOS src]$ git status -s
```

Git status is showing that the file has been reverted from the staging area.

```
[jerry@CentOS src]$ head -2 string_operations.c
#include <stdio.h>
```

The head command also shows that the reset operation removed the local changes too.

PART 16: GIT - TAG OPERATION

Tag operation allows giving meaningful names to a specific version in the repository. Suppose Tom and Jerry decide to tag their project code so that they can later access it easily.

Create Tags

Let us tag the current HEAD by using the git tag command. Tom provides a tag name with -a option and provides a tag message with –m option.

```
tom@CentOS project]$ pwd
/home/tom/top_repo/project
[tom@CentOS project]$ git tag -a 'Release_1_0' -m 'Tagged basic string operation code' HEAD
```

If you want to tag a particular commit, then use the appropriate COMMIT ID instead of the HEAD pointer. Tom uses the following command to push the tag into the remote repository.

```
[tom@CentOS project]$ git push origin tag Release_1_0
```

The above command will produce the following result —

```
Counting objects: 1, done.
Writing objects: 100% (1/1), 183 bytes, done.
Total 1 (delta 0), reused 0 (delta 0)
To gituser@git.server.com:project.git
* [new tag]
Release_1_0 -> Release_1_0
```

View Tags

Tom created tags. Now, Jerry can view all the available tags by using the Git tag command with –l option.

```
[jerry@CentOS src]$ pwd
/home/jerry/jerry_repo/project/src
[jerry@CentOS src]$ git pull
remote: Counting objects: 1, done.
remote: Total 1 (delta 0), reused 0 (delta 0)
Unpacking objects: 100% (1/1), done.
From git.server.com:project
* [new tag]
Release_1_0 -> Release_1_0
Current branch master is up to date.
[jerry@CentOS src]$ git tag -l
Release_1_0
```

Jerry uses the Git show command followed by its tag name to view more details about tag.

```
[jerry@CentOS src]$ git show Release_1_0
```

The above command will produce the following result —

```
tag Release_1_0
Tagger: Tom Cat <tom@tutorialspoint.com>
Date: Wed Sep 11 13:45:54 2013 +0530
Tagged basic string operation code
commit 577647211ed44fe2ae479427a0668a4f12ed71a1
Author: Tom Cat <tom@tutorialspoint.com>
Date: Wed Sep 11 10:21:20 2013 +0530
Removed executable binary
diff --git a/src/string_operations b/src/string_operations
deleted file mode 100755
index 654004b..0000000
Binary files a/src/string_operations and /dev/null differ
```

Delete Tags

Tom uses the following command to delete tags from the local as well as the remote repository.

```
[tom@CentOS project]$ git tag
Release_1_0
[tom@CentOS project]$ git tag -d Release_1_0
Deleted tag 'Release_1_0' (was 0f81ff4)
# Remove tag from remote repository.
[tom@CentOS project]$ git push origin :Release_1_0
To gituser@git.server.com:project.git
- [deleted]
Release_1_0
```

PART 17: GIT - PATCH OPERATION

Patch is a text file, whose contents are similar to Git diff, but along with code, it also has metadata about commits; e.g., commit ID, date, commit message, etc. We can create a patch from commits and other people can apply them to their repository.

Jerry implements the strcat function for his project. Jerry can create a path of his code and send it to Tom. Then, he can apply the received patch to his code.

Jerry uses the Git format-patch command to create a patch for the latest commit. If you want to create a patch for a specific commit, then use COMMIT_ID with the format-patch command.

```
[jerry@CentOS project]$ pwd
/home/jerry/jerry_repo/project/src
[jerry@CentOS src]$ git status -s
M string_operations.c
?? string_operations
[jerry@CentOS src]$ git add string_operations.c
[jerry@CentOS src]$ git commit -m "Added my_strcat function"
[master b4c7f09] Added my_strcat function
1 files changed, 13 insertions(+), 0 deletions(-)
[jerry@CentOS src]$ git format-patch -1
0001-Added-my_strcat-function.patch
```

The above command creates .patch files inside the current working directory. Tom can use this patch to modify his files. Git provides two commands to apply patches git amand git apply, respectively. Git apply modifies the local files without creating commit, while git am modifies the file and creates commit as well.
To apply patch and create commit, use the following command −

```
[tom@CentOS src]$ pwd
/home/tom/top_repo/project/src
[tom@CentOS src]$ git diff
[tom@CentOS src]$ git status -s
[tom@CentOS src]$ git apply 0001-Added-my_strcat-function.patch
[tom@CentOS src]$ git status -s
M string_operations.c
?? 0001-Added-my_strcat-function.patch
```
Th
e patch gets applied successfully, now we can view the modifications by using the git diff command.

```
[tom@CentOS src]$ git diff
```

The above command will produce the following result −

```
diff --git a/src/string_operations.c b/src/string_operations.c
index 8ab7f42..f282fcf 100644
--- a/src/string_operations.c
+++ b/src/string_operations.c
@@ -1,5 +1,16 @@
 #include <stdio.h>
+char *my_strcat(char *t, char *s)
diff --git a/src/string_operations.c b/src/string_operations.c
index 8ab7f42..f282fcf 100644
--- a/src/string_operations.c
+++ b/src/string_operations.c
@@ -1,5 +1,16 @@
 #include <stdio.h>
+char *my_strcat(char *t, char *s)
+
 {
+
 char *p = t;
+
+
+
 while (*p)
 ++p;
+
 while (*p++ = *s++)
+ ;
+ return t;
+
 }
+
 size_t my_strlen(const char *s)
 {
 const char *p = s;
@@ -23,6 +34,7 @@ int main(void)
 {
```

PART 18: GIT - MANAGING BRANCHES

Branch operation allows creating another line of development. We can use this operation to fork off the development process into two different directions. For example, we released a product for 6.0 version and we might want to create a branch so that the development of 7.0 features can be kept separate from 6.0 bug fixes.

Create Branch

Tom creates a new branch using the git branch <branch name> command. We can create a new branch from an existing one. We can use a specific commit or tag as the starting point. If any specific commit ID is not provided, then the branch will be created with HEAD as its starting point.

```
[jerry@CentOS src]$ git branch new_branch
[jerry@CentOS src]$ git branch
* master
  new_branch
```

A new branch is created; Tom used the git branch command to list the available branches. Git shows an asterisk mark before currently checked out branch.
The pictorial representation of create branch operation is shown below −

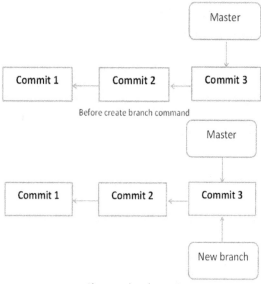

Before create branch command

After create branch operation

Switch between Branches

Jerry uses the git checkout command to switch between branches.

```
[jerry@CentOS src]$ git checkout new_branch
Switched to branch 'new_branch'
[jerry@CentOS src]$ git branch
master
* new_branch
```

Shortcut to Create and Switch Branch

In the above example, we have used two commands to create and switch branches, respectively. Git provides –b option with the checkout command; this operation creates a new branch and immediately switches to the new branch.

```
[jerry@CentOS src]$ git checkout -b test_branch
Switched to a new branch 'test_branch'
[jerry@CentOS src]$ git branch
master
new_branch
* test_branch
```

Delete a Branch

A branch can be deleted by providing –D option with git branch command. But before deleting the existing branch, switch to the other branch.

Jerry is currently on test_branch and he wants to remove that branch. So he switches branch and deletes branch as shown below.

```
[jerry@CentOS src]$ git branch
master
new_branch
* test_branch
[jerry@CentOS src]$ git checkout master
Switched to branch 'master'
[jerry@CentOS src]$ git branch -D test_branch
Deleted branch test_branch (was 5776472).
```

Now, Git will show only two branches.

```
[jerry@CentOS src]$ git branch
* master
new_branch
```

Rename a Branch

Jerry decides to add support for wide characters in his string operations project. He has already created a new branch, but the branch name is not appropriate. So he changes the branch name by using –m option followed by the old branch name and the new branch name.

```
[jerry@CentOS src]$ git branch
* master
new_branch
[jerry@CentOS src]$ git branch -m new_branch wchar_support
Now, the git branch command will show the new branch name.
[jerry@CentOS src]$ git branch
* master
wchar_support
```

Merge Two Branches

Jerry implements a function to return the string length of wide character string.
New the code will appear as follows —

```
[jerry@CentOS src]$ git branch
master
* wchar_support
[jerry@CentOS src]$ pwd
/home/jerry/jerry_repo/project/src
[jerry@CentOS src]$ git diff
```

The above command produces the following result —

```
t a/src/string_operations.c b/src/string_operations.c
index 8ab7f42..8fb4b00 100644
--- a/src/string_operations.c
+++ b/src/string_operations.c
@@ -1,4 +1,14 @@
#include <stdio.h>
+#include <wchar.h>
+
+size_t w_strlen(const wchar_t *s)
+
{
 +
 const wchar_t *p = s;
 +
 +
 while (*p)
 + ++p;
 + return (p - s);
 +
}
```

After testing, he commits and pushes his changes to the new branch.

```
[jerry@CentOS src]$ git status -s
M string_operations.c
?? string_operations
[jerry@CentOS src]$ git add string_operations.c
[jerry@CentOS src]$ git commit -m 'Added w_strlen function to return string lenght of wchar_t
string'
[wchar_support 64192f9] Added w_strlen function to return string lenght of wchar_t string
1 files changed, 10 insertions(+), 0 deletions(-)
```

Note that Jerry is pushing these changes to the new branch, which is why he used
the branch name wchar_support instead of master branch.

```
[jerry@CentOS src]$ git push origin wchar_support   <--- Observer branch_name
```

The above command will produce the following result.

```
Counting objects: 7, done.
Compressing objects: 100% (4/4), done.
Writing objects: 100% (4/4), 507 bytes, done.
Total 4 (delta 1), reused 0 (delta 0)
To gituser@git.server.com:project.git
* [new branch]
wchar_support -> wchar_support
```

After committing the changes, the new branch will appear as follows —

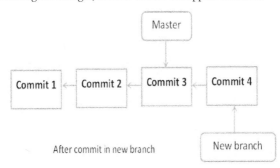

After commit in new branch

Tom is curious about what Jerry is doing in his private branch and he checks the log from the wchar_support branch.

```
[tom@CentOS src]$ pwd
/home/tom/top_repo/project/src
[tom@CentOS src]$ git log origin/wchar_support -2
```

The above command will produce the following result.

```
commit 64192f91d7cc2bcdf3bf946dd33ece63b74184a3
Author: Jerry Mouse <jerry@tutorialspoint.com>
Date: Wed Sep 11 16:10:06 2013 +0530
Added w_strlen function to return string lenght of wchar_t string
commit 577647211ed44fe2ae479427a0668a4f12ed71a1
Author: Tom Cat <tom@tutorialspoint.com>
Date: Wed Sep 11 10:21:20 2013 +0530
Removed executable binary
```

By viewing commit messages, Tom realizes that Jerry implemented the strlen function for wide character and he wants the same functionality in the master branch. Instead of re-implementing, he decides to take Jerry's code by merging his branch with the master branch.

```
[tom@CentOS project]$ git branch
* master
[tom@CentOS project]$ pwd
/home/tom/top_repo/project
[tom@CentOS project]$ git merge origin/wchar_support
Updating 5776472..64192f9
Fast-forward
src/string_operations.c | 10 ++++++++++
1 files changed, 10 insertions(+), 0 deletions(-)
```

After the merge operation, the master branch will appear as follows —

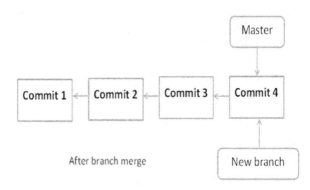

After branch merge

Now, the branch wchar_support has been merged with the master branch. We can verify it by viewing the commit message or by viewing the modifications done into the string operation.c file.

```
[tom@CentOS project]$ cd src/
[tom@CentOS src]$ git log -1
commit 64192f91d7cc2bcdf3bf946dd33ece63b74184a3
Author:JerryMouse
Date:WedSep1116:10:062013+0530
    Added w_strlen function to returnstring lenght ofwchar_tstring
[tom@CentOS src]$ head -12 string_operations.c
```

The above command will produce the following result.

```
#include <stdio.h>
#include <wchar.h>
size_t w_strlen(const wchar_t *s)
{
 const wchar_t *p = s;
 while (*p)
 ++p;
 return (p - s);
}
```

After testing, he pushes his code changes to the master branch.

```
[tom@CentOS src]$ git push origin master
Total0(delta 0), reused 0(delta 0)
To gituser@git.server.com:project.git
5776472..64192f9 master -> master
```

Rebase Branches

The Git rebase command is a branch merge command, but the difference is that it modifies the order of commits.

The Git merge command tries to put the commits from other branches on top of the HEAD of the current local branch. For example, your local branch has commits A->B->C->D and the merge branch has commits A->B->X->Y, then git merge will convert the current local branch to something like A->B->C->D->X->Y

The Git rebase command tries to find out the common ancestor between the current local branch and the merge branch. It then pushes the commits to the local branch by modifying the order of commits in the current local branch. For example, if your local branch has commits A->B->C->D and the merge branch has commits A->B->X->Y, then Git rebase will convert the current local branch to something like A->B->X->Y->C->D.

When multiple developers work on a single remote repository, you cannot modify the order of the commits in the remote repository. In this situation, you can use rebase operation to put your local commits on top of the remote repository commits and you can push these changes.

PART 19: GIT - HANDLING CONFLICTS

Perform Changes in wchar_support Branch

Jerry is working on the wchar_support branch. He changes the name of the functions and after testing, he commits his changes.

```
[jerry@CentOS src]$ git branch
  master
* wchar_support
[jerry@CentOS src]$ git diff
```

The above command produces the following result —

```
diff --git a/src/string_operations.c b/src/string_operations.c
index 8fb4b00..01ff4e0 100644
--- a/src/string_operations.c
+++ b/src/string_operations.c
@@ -1,7 +1,7 @@
#include <stdio.h>
#include <wchar.h>
-size_t w_strlen(const wchar_t *s)
+size_t my_wstrlen(const wchar_t *s)
{
  const wchar_t *p = s;
```

After verifying the code he commits his changes.

```
[jerry@CentOS src]$ git status -s
M string_operations.c
[jerry@CentOS src]$ git add string_operations.c
[jerry@CentOS src]$ git commit -m 'Changed function name'
[wchar_support 3789fe8] Changed function name
1 files changed, 1 insertions(+), 1 deletions(-)
[jerry@CentOS src]$ git push origin wchar_support
```

The above command will produce the following result —

```
Counting objects: 7, done.
Compressing objects: 100% (4/4), done.
Writing objects: 100% (4/4), 409 bytes, done.
Total 4 (delta 1), reused 0 (delta 0)
To gituser@git.server.com:project.git
64192f9..3789fe8 wchar_support -> wchar_support
```

Perform Changes in Master Branch

Meanwhile in the master branch, Tom also changes the name of the same function and pushes his changes to the master branch.

```
[tom@CentOS src]$ git branch
* master
[tom@CentOS src]$ git diff
```

The above command produces the following result —

```
diff --git a/src/string_operations.c b/src/string_operations.c
index 8fb4b00..52bec84 100644
--- a/src/string_operations.c
+++ b/src/string_operations.c
@@ -1,7 +1,8 @@
#include <stdio.h>
#include <wchar.h>
-size_t w_strlen(const wchar_t *s)
+/* wide character strlen fucntion */
+size_t my_wc_strlen(const wchar_t *s)
{
  const wchar_t *p = s;
```

After verifying diff, he commits his changes.

```
[tom@CentOS src]$ git status -s
M string_operations.c
[tom@CentOS src]$ git add string_operations.c
[tom@CentOS src]$ git commit -m 'Changed function name from w_strlen to my_wc_strlen'
[master ad4b530] Changed function name from w_strlen to my_wc_strlen
1 files changed, 2 insertions(+), 1 deletions(-)
[tom@CentOS src]$ git push origin master
```

The above command will produce the following result –

```
Counting objects: 7, done.
Compressing objects: 100% (4/4), done.
Writing objects: 100% (4/4), 470 bytes, done.
Total 4 (delta 1), reused 0 (delta 0)
To gituser@git.server.com:project.git
64192f9..ad4b530 master -> master
```

On the wchar_support branch, Jerry implements strchr function for wide character string. After testing, he commits and pushes his changes to the wchar_support branch.

```
[jerry@CentOS src]$ git branch
master
* wchar_support
[jerry@CentOS src]$ git diff
```

The above command produces the following result –

```
diff --git a/src/string_operations.c b/src/string_operations.c
index 01ff4e0..163a779 100644
--- a/src/string_operations.c
+++ b/src/string_operations.c
@@ -1,6 +1,16 @@
#include <stdio.h>
#include <wchar.h>
+wchar_t *my_wstrchr(wchar_t *ws, wchar_t wc)
+
{
+
 while (*ws)
 {
+
 if (*ws == wc)
+
 return ws;
+
 ++ws;
+
 }
+ return NULL;
+
}
+
size_t my_wstrlen(const wchar_t *s)
{
 const wchar_t *p = s;
```

After verifying, he commits his changes.

```
[jerry@CentOS src]$ git status -s
M string_operations.c
[jerry@CentOS src]$ git add string_operations.c
[jerry@CentOS src]$ git commit -m 'Addded strchr function for wide character string'
[wchar_support 9d201a9] Addded strchr function for wide character string
1 files changed, 10 insertions(+), 0 deletions(-)
[jerry@CentOS src]$ git push origin wchar_support
```

The above command will produce the following result −

```
Counting objects: 7, done.
Compressing objects: 100% (4/4), done.
Writing objects: 100% (4/4), 516 bytes, done.
Total 4 (delta 1), reused 0 (delta 0)
To gituser@git.server.com:project.git
3789fe8..9d201a9 wchar_support -> wchar_support
```

Tackle Conflicts

Tom wants to see what Jerry is doing on his private branch so, he tries to pull the latest changes from the wchar_support branch, but Git aborts the operation with the following error message.

```
[tom@CentOS src]$ git pull origin wchar_support
```

The above command produces the following result −

```
remote: Counting objects: 11, done.
63Git Tutorials
remote: Compressing objects: 100% (8/8), done.
remote: Total 8 (delta 2), reused 0 (delta 0)
Unpacking objects: 100% (8/8), done.
From git.server.com:project
 * branch
wchar_support -> FETCH_HEAD
Auto-merging src/string_operations.c
CONFLICT (content): Merge conflict in src/string_operations.c
Automatic merge failed; fix conflicts and then commit the result.
```

Resolve Conflicts

From the error message, it is clear that there is a conflict in
src/string_operations.c . He runs the git diff command to view further details.

```
[tom@CentOS src]$ git diff
```

The above command produces the following result −

```
diff --cc src/string_operations.c
index 52bec84,163a779..0000000
--- a/src/string_operations.c
+++ b/src/string_operations.c
@@@ -1,8 -1,17 +1,22 @@@
#include <stdio.h>
#include <wchar.h>
++<<<<<<< HEAD
+/* wide character strlen fucntion */
+size_t my_wc_strlen(const wchar_t *s)
++=======
+ wchar_t *my_wstrchr(wchar_t *ws, wchar_t wc)
+
{
 +
 +
while (*ws)
{
if (*ws == wc)
+
return ws;
+
++ws;
+
}
+ return NULL;
 +
}
+
+ size_t my_wstrlen(const wchar_t *s)
++>>>>>>>9d201a9c61bc4713f4095175f8954b642dae8f86
{
 const wchar_t *p = s;
```

As both Tom and Jerry changed the name of the same function, Git is in a state
of confusion and it asks the user to resolve the conflict manually.

Tom decides to keep the function name suggested by Jerry, but he keeps the
comment added by him, as it is. After removing the conflict markers, git diff will
look like this.

```
[tom@CentOS src]$ git diff
```

The above command produces the following result.

```
diff --cc src/string_operations.c
diff --cc src/string_operations.c
index 52bec84,163a779..0000000
--- a/src/string_operations.c
+++ b/src/string_operations.c
@@@ -1,8 -1,17 +1,18 @@@
#include <stdio.h>
#include <wchar.h>
+ wchar_t *my_wstrchr(wchar_t *ws, wchar_t wc)
+
{
+
 while (*ws)
 {
+
 if (*ws == wc)
+
 return ws;
+
 ++ws;
+
 }
+ return NULL;
+
}
+
+/* wide character strlen fucntion */
- size_t my_wc_strlen(const wchar_t *s)
+ size_t my_wstrlen(const wchar_t *s)
{
 const wchar_t *p = s;
```

As Tom has modified the files, he has to commit these changes first and thereafter, he can pull the changes.

```
[tom@CentOS src]$ git commit -a -m 'Resolved conflict'
[master 6b1ac36] Resolved conflict
[tom@CentOS src]$ git pull origin wchar_support.
```

Tom has resolved the conflict, now the pull operation will succeed.

PART 20: GIT - DIFFERENT PLATFORMS

GNU/Linux and Mac OS uses line-feed (LF), or new line as line ending character, while Windows uses line-feed and carriage-return (LFCR) combination to represent the line-ending character.

To avoid unnecessary commits because of these line-ending differences, we have to configure the Git client to write the same line ending to the Git repository.

For Windows system, we can configure the Git client to convert line endings to CRLF format while checking out, and convert them back to LF format during the commit operation. The following settings will do the needful.

```
[tom@CentOS project]$ git config --global core.autocrlf true
```

For GNU/Linux or Mac OS, we can configure the Git client to convert line endings from CRLF to LF while performing the checkout operation.

```
[tom@CentOS project]$ git config --global core.autocrlf input
```

PART 21: GIT - ONLINE REPOSITORIES

GitHub is a web-based hosting service for software development projects that uses the Git revision control system. It also has their standard GUI application available for download (Windows, Mac, GNU/ Linux) directly from the service's website. But in this session, we will see only CLI part.

Create GitHub Repository

Go to github.com. If you already have the GitHub account, then login using that account or create a new one. Follow the steps from github.com website to create a new repository.

Push Operation

Tom decides to use the GitHub server. To start a new project, he creates a new directory and one file inside that.

```
[tom@CentOS]$ mkdir github_repo
[tom@CentOS]$ cd github_repo/
[tom@CentOS]$ vi hello.c
[tom@CentOS]$ make hello
cc hello.c -o hello
[tom@CentOS]$ ./hello
```

The above command will produce the following result:

```
                         Hello, World !!!
```

After verifying his code, he initializes the directory with the git init command and commits his changes locally.

```
[tom@CentOS]$ git init
Initialized empty Git repository in /home/tom/github_repo/.git/
[tom@CentOS]$ git status -s
?? hello
?? hello.c
[tom@CentOS]$ git add hello.c
[tom@CentOS]$ git status -s
A hello.c
?? hello
[tom@CentOS]$ git commit -m 'Initial commit'
```

After that, he adds the GitHub repository URL as a remote origin and pushes his changes to the remote repository.

```
[tom@CentOS]$ git remote add origin https://github.com/kangralkar/testing_repo.git
[tom@CentOS]$ git push -u origin master
```

Push operation will ask for GitHub user name and password. After successful authentication, the operation will succeed.

The above command will produce the following result:

```
Username for 'https://github.com': kangralkar
Password for 'https://kangralkar@github.com':
Counting objects: 3, done.
Writing objects: 100% (3/3), 214 bytes, done.
Total 3 (delta 0), reused 0 (delta 0)
To https://github.com/kangralkar/test_repo.git
 * [new branch] master -> master
 Branch master set up to track remote branch master from origin.
```

From now, Tom can push any changes to the GitHub repository. He can use all the commands discussed in this chapter with the GitHub repository.

Pull Operation

Tom successfully pushed all his changes to the GitHub repository. Now, other developers can view these changes by performing clone operation or updating their local repository.

Jerry creates a new directory in his home directory and clones the GitHub repository by using the git clone command.

```
[jerry@CentOS]$ pwd
/home/jerry
[jerry@CentOS]$ mkdir jerry_repo
[jerry@CentOS]$ git clone https://github.com/kangralkar/test_repo.git
```

The above command produces the following result:

```
Cloning into 'test_repo'...
remote: Counting objects: 3, done.
remote: Total 3 (delta 0), reused 3 (delta 0)
Unpacking objects: 100% (3/3), done.
```

He verifies the directory contents by executing the ls command.

```
[jerry@CentOS]$ ls
test_repo
[jerry@CentOS]$ ls test_repo/
hello.c
```